# Core Bazel

## Fast Builds For Busy People

### Bogdan Mustiata

# Table of Contents

Cover image taken from: https://www.pexels.com/de-de/foto/ aufnahme-von-unten-aufzug-ausrustung-bau-2068478/

# Chapter 1. Intro

This book is intended to get you up to speed with Bazel as fast as humanly possible. Bazel is a fast, scalable, multi-language, and extensible build system built by Google to address their needs, namely building large software written in multiple languages, for various platforms, as fast as possible. Bazel can scale from mini-projects to insanely large projects with ease, making it extremely appealing to projects.

This book starts with the premise you have no idea what Bazel is, so everything discussed will be explained *concisely* and *structured* in the following pages.

Since you're a busy person, we're not going to gloss over obvious things - such as installing it on your platform or running Bazel from the command line. I believe these things are better covered in the documentation anyway, so it would be redundant to have them here.

Instead, we'll focus on the *essentials*: How does Bazel work internally? How do we create and extend Bazel builds?

This way, if you just picked this book up, you should be able to get into Bazel in a matter of hours by reading this book and have a rather solid understanding of its core concepts.

The idea is to get you to the point where when you'll see a new project, you'll be able to find what's going on, and where to look to find more information when you won't know some things. If you have to continue some project build or implement the build system from scratch, you'll have the mindset and the tools to do so.

You'll see from time to time some symbols, with a short text. The following symbols have these meanings:

 This indicates something you should probably do when creating your builds.

 This abbreviates a more complex idea, into a digestible nugget.

 You should pay attention to this when writing your builds, or you might run into serious trouble.

Inlined code will appear as such: `bazel build`

*Important things* will be *written in italic*.

All the code discussed here is available at https://github.com/bmustiata/bazel-samples

Any updates to the text you'll get for free in the electronic version of this document.

Let's start!

# Chapter 2. Basic Bazel

# 2.1. Action Graph

Bazel builds software, and it's very-very efficient at doing that.

To achieve that, it works by constructing a graph. It starts from the source files and uses *actions* to transform the source files into intermediary outputs, and in the end, into the final artifacts.

An *action* is the smallest unit of work that we'll have available in our graph that transforms some input files into some output files, or in the case no input files are needed, produces only output files. Despite its fancy name, an action is just a node in a graph, denoting a program execution, with its arguments, environment, such as `javac` or `gcc`:

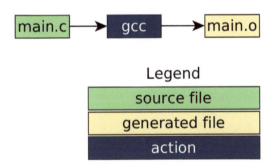

*This action graph idea is the essential concept you need to understand from Bazel.* All we will do in Bazel is constructing this graph. When running builds, Bazel will pick subpaths from the graph, then traverse them for the actual selection and execution of actions.

An action is a program execution that must have at least one output file.

Bazel uses a language very similar to Python to build this graph. This programming language is called Skylark. All the code we'll write in terms of the Bazel build code is Skylark code.

So. How does everything happen? Bazel will run everything in three phases:

1. First, it will load all the scripts we have written. This section is called the *loading phase*.

2. Then, it will execute the scripts that create the graph. This second phase is called the *analysis phase*. The result at the end of this is just the graph in memory. No action has executed yet.

3. Lastly, Bazel selects the path inside the graph needed to build what we want to be built. It then traverses the graph, running the configured actions. This is the *execution phase*.

 Analysis means the graph building in Bazel parlance.

After it builds the graph (analysis), Bazel looks at what part of it needs to run, it creates an empty sandbox folder, and executes the actions mapped against that folder. The sandbox folder starts empty, so no files from the project can be accessed unless they were explicitly made accessible as inputs in the graph.

This explicit input declaration is to guarantee that caching, and remote execution will work correctly. Bazel will copy only the files declared inside the folder.

To have something concrete to follow, we'll start with a basic C sample. In this project we have `main.c` that's the main program, and `print.h` and `print.c` that allow us to print formatted text on the screen. If we would have a simple C project, we might build a graph looking something like this; assuming we want to compile it and create a zipped artifact as output:

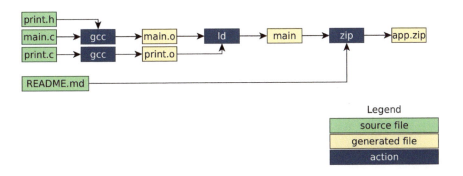

We start from source files. We tell Bazel that each source file should be transformed into another generated file, describing how this happens using actions. An action links the input files (if any), with its outputs, and specify what program needs to run to get from those input files, the output files. Actions can generate multiple files, but they must create at least one file, since Bazel doesn't support actions without any side effects on the filesytem.

 You cannot have folders as inputs or outputs for actions.

As you can notice, Bazel needs mapping every single intermediary file as well. Bazel doesn't support folders as inputs. All the input files, and all the intermediary files must be specified. This approach has some significant advantages.

Analyzing this graph, Bazel can do speed optimizations, such as running the build in parallel or skipping unnecessary steps.

Bazel also holds an extremely aggressive cache of all the intermediary outputs, by hashing them. So if only the `print.c` file gets changed, and a new build runs, Bazel analyzes the graph and does only the required steps, skipping quite a few compilation actions:

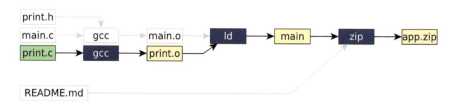

But what happens if in the `print.c` file we only change a comment? The compilation using gcc will yield the same binary output for the print.o. What happens then:

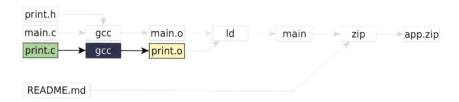

Bazel infers it's unnecessary to run the rest of the execution graph. It knows that down the line, the output will be the same, by just looking at the cached hashes of the files.

To have a Bazel build, we will need to define the graph of source files, with its transforming actions - basically what programs we want to run, and output files.

Bazel was build from day 1 to support huge repositories. To make the builds rock-solid, fast, cacheable, and scalable, Bazel introduces quite a few concepts and limitations on what can be done inside the builds. These constructs can prove very frustrating if we don't understand the concepts with which Bazel operates.

To introduce these concepts, we'll start small, expanding on the ideas to get a gradual inset of why things are the way they are. This knowledge will allow us to reason why aren't things working and how to structure our builds, so they are rock-solid, fast, cacheable, and scalable.

# 2.2. Rules and Targets

We can't call actions directly. Bazel doesn't permit simple action invocations. We can't just invoke a shell script. Special functions called *rules* define the actions to be invoked. A rule is a reusable function and is the smallest building block allowed by Bazel that enables us to stitch actions together.

A rule is a function that stitches a part of the graph.

Since rules themselves are functions, i.e., code building the graph, the actual invocation of that function, with all its parameters defining what needs construction, is called a *target* in this context.

 A target is a named rule invocation.

(Now, honestly speaking, targets can also be files used in `BUILD` files, or package groups, but for the sake of simplicity, we'll skip these for now.)

Since targets are named function invocations, each rule has a parameter called *name* that identifies its instance.

I know it sounds complicated, but the only thing you need remembering for now is that *a rule is a function*, and *a target is a function call*.

To make it even more definite, we'll break this chapter in two:

First, we'll start with a single package that contains only one rule - the archiving rule. We'll have a small sample that can build three archives.

In the second part, we'll also see the rules to compile, link, and do minor refactors on top of the archiving rule, as our understanding of what rules are and what they can do expanded.

# 2.2.1. Archiving Rule

As promised, we start with our simple rule, and we expand on what targets and rules are with this concrete sample. Here we'll start with a basic project that all it does, is to archive files together.

Before we start, we should mention two files that will be present in our folder:

1. A file called `WORKSPACE`, that will be an empty file for the time being, and is just a marker for Bazel that this *is* a Bazel *project*.

2. A file called `BUILD`, that defines a *package*, where our targets will be defined.

Don't worry, we'll address them in more depth later, but now, let's just focus on rules and targets.

## 2.2.1.1. Targets

Let's assume we already have written our rule called `archive`. We'll write the code for it immediately, don't fret. This rule (function) has two parameters:

1. `files` - that defines the files to be archived,
2. `out` - that defines the output file name of the archive.

Thus we could have several targets (rule invocations) for this archive rule in our BUILD file:

```
load(":bazel/archive.bzl", "archive")  ①

archive(
  name="documentation",  ②
  files=[
    "src/README.md",
  ],
  out="documentation.zip",
)

archive(
  name="release",  ③
  files=[
    "src/RELEASE.md",
  ],
  out="release.zip",
)

archive(
  name="all",  ④
  files=[
    "src/README.md",
    "src/RELEASE.md",
  ],
  out="all.zip",
)
```

① We load the rule into the current scope. We'll show the rule code in the next section.

② The *documentation* target,

③ the *release* target,

④ and the *all* target.

We can see that we're having three invocations of the rule, and each one creates a distinct target: *documentation*, *release*, and *all*. The different names identify each rule invocation. Each target *must have a* `name` *attribute* to identify it, and all identifiers must be unique in the package.

So Bazel starts its loading phase, where all the scripts are initially loaded, then the analysis happens where the graph is assembled. It is in this *analysis phase*, when Bazel *invokes the rules* and creates these targets.

With the graph in hand, Bazel will look at what needs to execute to get the targets' outputs. It does that looking at the actions required, analyze them against its cache, and run only the ones for which no outputs are already cached.

With our three targets defined, we could tell Bazel to build only one or more of them:

```
bazel build documentation release all
```

This command is the last piece of the lifecycle puzzle. This command tells Bazel it's supposed to build three targets. So after the code is loaded, the graph is built (analysis phase). Bazel looks at what the rule defines as outputs, and starts backtracking the graph, to see what it would need to execute to get from the sources to the specified outputs. In the build phase, only the part of the graph needed gets built.

What if run only `bazel build release`? Even if the graph has the *documentation* and *all* targets, the actions defined to get those targets won't get executed since they are not required. Only what's necessary for the outputs of the *release* target will run.

## 2.2.1.2. Rules

A rule is a function with parameters that will stitch several actions together, fastening together files with their corresponding generating actions. Rules are the building blocks that we assemble to make our builds happen.

So rules are just functions that prescribe actions chained together to build the outputs we want. Notice that when talking about rules, I used the wording "prescribe actions." Whenever you will see code such as:

```
ctx.actions.run(
    executable="zip",
    arguments=[args],
    inputs=ctx.files.files,
    outputs=[out_file])
```

It doesn't mean the action will instantly get called. Invoking the actions method is merely adding a node into the graph, not an actual program execution. It solely instructs Bazel to run the given command only if one of the outputs was requested, and we're not already hitting the cache.

 `ctx.actions.run` just adds a node in the graph, even if the name might imply something else.

With this in mind, let's finally look at the full code of our *archive* rule, we set ourselves up to create in the `bazel/archive.bzl`:

```
def _archive(ctx):   ①
  out_file = ctx.actions.declare_file(ctx.attr.out)
  args = ctx.actions.args()

  args.add(out_file)
  args.add_all(ctx.files.files)   ⑤

  ctx.actions.run(
     executable="zip",
     arguments=[args],
     inputs=ctx.files.files,
     outputs=[out_file])

  return [DefaultInfo(files=depset([out_file]))]   ⑥

archive = rule(   ②
  implementation = _archive,
  attrs = {   ③
     "files": attr.label_list(allow_files=True),   ④
     "out": attr.string(mandatory=True),
  }
)
```

① This is the full code that implements our rule. This function has a single parameter, the rule context.

② To register a new rule definition, we call the native function named `rule`. This call registers our rule with Bazel and defines the arguments of our rule.

③ The available arguments to the rule must be specified in this `args` dictionary.

④ Arguments are created typed. Use the implicit module `attr` to declare the type definitions.

⑤ The parameters are also available in the context, and with them, the actions are created and stitched together.

⑥ The rule defines what outputs will be generated by itself

 If the rule doesn't define any outputs, the actions don't execute. Bazel always analyses the graph for what actions to run.

So the most obvious thing you've probably already noticed is that a rule has two parts:

1. *the rule declaration* into Bazel,

2. and the actual *code that implements the rule*.

In our previous example, we can see the rule declaration here:

```
archive = rule(    ①
    implementation = _archive,    ②
    attrs = {    ③
        "files": attr.label_list(allow_files=True),    ④
    }
)
```

① Rule declaration.

② Reference to the implementation.

③ A dictionary comprising all the parameters our rule accepts.

④ Each entry defines the parameter name and type, including

extra constraints such as if it's required or not, default values, etc.

The call to the native `rule` function registers the function into Bazel. This registration happens during the loading phase. This call records the rule named *"archive"* (1) with its implementation `_archive` (2) and the parameters (3) into Bazel.

When declaring the parameters, Bazel requires defining the types of parameters (4). When the analysis phase executes later, it will furthermore enforce the arguments' constraints when invoking the rules, and if they don't match, the Bazel build will fail.

# 2.2.2. load statement

Let's take a quick break and introduce the `load` statement in a bit more depth before we go further. This is a statement we'll use extensively.

How it works is rather simple:

```
load("@//path/to/package:file.bzl", "rule_name")
```

The first parameter is a *label* pointing to the file from where we're loading the rule. You'll find more about labels in the *Packages and Workspaces* section. Just note that the first part is a path to a package, in our sample, the current root folder.

The next parameters are names that we want to import from

that file. Note that we can import multiple names simultaneously:

```
load("@//path/to/package:file.bzl", "rule_name",
"other_rule")
```

and that we can alias the name we want to import with a different name, using a rather peculiar syntax:

```
load("@//path/to/package:file.bzl", "rule_name",
aliased_rule="other_rule")
```

After this `load` we have now two rules:

1. `rule_name`
2. `aliased_rule` (this is still `other_rule` in the `file.bzl`)

These `load` statements are the Python equivalent of:

```
from package_name import rule_name
```

And

```
from package_name import other_rule as aliased_rule
```

# 2.2.3. Rule Inputs and Outputs

Now with a simple rule done, let's look at how rules look in general, such as the compiling rule:

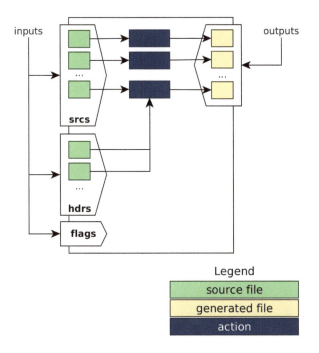

Legend

| |
|---|
| source file |
| generated file |
| action |

In this case, the sources, the headers, and eventual build parameters are the input parameters for our rule - the `attr` attribute in the `rule` call.

Inside this rule, we'll iterate over each input file, and create an action to compile that file. The output of the action will be an object file:

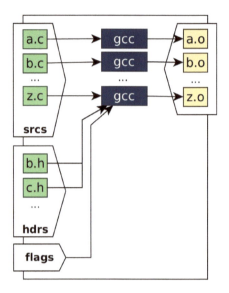

We do this for the same reason we discussed in the previous section: we want to leverage Bazel's graph system to do the caching and speed optimizations for us.

We could feed everything to `gcc`:

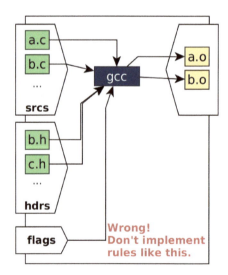

However, this has the drawback of running the recompilation of everything, even if only a single source has changed.

For linking, we'll do the same thing:

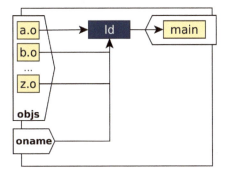

Then we will archive everything, using yet another rule:

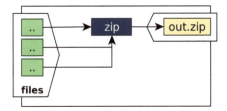

And this is the way we'll combine them eventually:

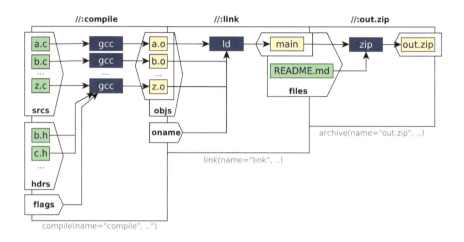

I've added at the top our targets because now you understand how this goes down. Don't forget that if we remove all the clutter with input and output parameters and rule invocations, Bazel will see this as an action graph:

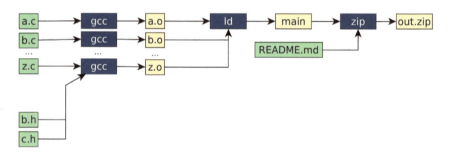

Pretty neat, isn't it? So let's go back to our rules' inputs and outputs.

## 2.2.3.1. Rule Context

If you're a Python programmer, you've noticed already there's a bunch of shady things going around here. There are no imports.

None. Nada.

The code for the rule definition itself doesn't have *any* imports at all.

As you have noticed on each rule written, there's one single parameter defined in the rule implementation, and that is the rule context. This argument is a God object that contains almost everything you'll need:

1. parameters passed into the rule, that are further broken down in different structures (`ctx.file…` - for single files, `ctx.files…` for multiple files, or `ctx.attr…` for regular parameters) depending on the type,

2. modules to add actions to the graph - `ctx.actions`, or to build action arguments `ctx.args`,

3. input files that are processed by Bazel, even before starting the build, (you'll see them later in the *External Data*)

4. variables that maybe were set upstream in the graph, and you can now use, or also export your variables to downstream rules.

I'm pretty sure that even with this list, I'm missing something.

 To see the list of all the attributes you can run `print(dir(ctx))`, or read its documentation [https://docs.bazel.build/versions/master/skylark/lib/ctx.html].

The variables we defined, and we registered using the `rule` function, are available in the context's `attr` field. Depending on the type of the variable, regular attribute, or file, it might also be present in one of the other substructures of the context:

- `file` - When the attribute defines a single file possible by having for example in the `attr` parameter dictionary an entry such as `"out":` `attr.label(allow_single_file=True)`. Python-wise `ctx.file` is somewhat the equivalent of a `Dict[str, File]` type.

- `files` - When the attribute defines an array of files possible i.e. `"files": attr.label_list(allow_files=True)`. Python-wise `ctx.files` is the equivalent of a `Dict[str,` `List[File]]`.

 We can use `ctx.file.param_name` to access single files, or `ctx.files.param_name` to access lists of files.

If the attributes are defined as files, they're still visible under the `attr`, but only the ones available under the `ctx.file` or `ctx.files` attributes will allow us to use them as dependencies for actions:

```
ctx.actions.run(
  executable="zip",
  arguments=[args],
  inputs=ctx.files.files,
  outputs=[out_file])
```

Here we're defining the inputs as *all the files* specified in the
`files` attribute.

But the keen observers, from you, have seen now that there's
nowhere defined `DefaultInfo` nor `depset` :

```
return [DefaultInfo(files=depset([out_file]))]  ⑥
```

That's because Bazel defines them automagically in the context
of the rule.

That last "return" brings us to our next topic:

# 2.2.3.2. Rule return (Providers)

I am sure the following line of code is difficult to parse by a
normal human being, that doesn't have any previous exposure to
Bazel:

```
return [DefaultInfo(files=depset([out_file]))]  ⑥
```

To understand what it means, we need to go back to our
previous diagram that showed our compilation:

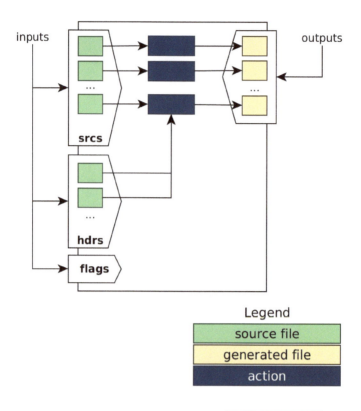

inputs

outputs

**srcs**

**hdrs**

**flags**

Legend

| source file |
| generated file |
| action |

The *outputs* you see in here is the `DefaultInfo` object instance added here. If the return is not defined, our graph looks like this, and then no action executes:

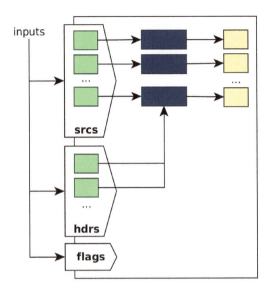

Why? Because Bazel can't find a `DefaultInfo` object to extract the files out of it and to start backtracking the graph and mark the needed actions to be performed.

We had a warning before, but let me repeat it here:

 If the rule doesn't define any outputs, the actions don't execute. Bazel always analyses the graph for what actions to run.

So why is the result a list? In Bazel, a rule can return other data for the next targets in the chain. Since that's possible, this is why there's a list returned. We can return multiple results that are usable in downstream rules:

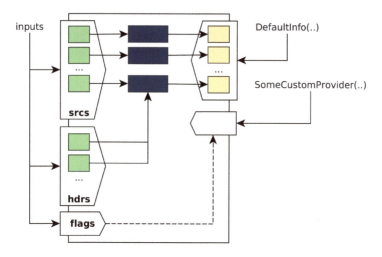

Each item in this list is called a `provider`, and you can even create your custom providers for your rules. Bazel itself comes with a bunch of providers [https://docs.bazel.build/versions/3.1.0/skylark/lib/skylark-provider.html]. These providers bundled in Bazel handle things such as passing variables, configurations for make projects, etc. from one rule to another.

You can also create a custom one using the `provider` function. To do that we simply call the `provider()` function:

```
Counter = provider()
```

This line of code creates a structure that can hold anything we want. Then we can have it as part of the return into our rules.

```
load("//:bazel/counter.bzl", "Counter")   ①

def _count_items(ctx):
    item_count = len(ctx.attr.items)     ②
    return [Counter(count=item_count)]   ③

count_items = rule(
  implementation = _count_items,
  attrs = {
    "items": attr.int_list(),
  }
)
```

① In this example, we have the `Counter` provider in its file, so we're loading it from there.

② We just count how many items we have in a list.

③ We store them in our provider. A custom provider can have any fields. We could also have `Counter(count=item_count, some_str="yay")`, etc.

> ℹ️ A custom provider can have any fields we assign to it.

Then we can refer to it into another rule, that simply displays the field from the provider received from the previous target:

```
load("//:bazel/counter.bzl", "Counter")

def _print_count(ctx):
  rule_dep = ctx.attr.rule_dep
  print(rule_dep[Counter])

  # we can also access the items from the struct
  directly:
  print("Count is {}".format(rule_dep[Counter].count))

  return []

print_count = rule(
  implementation = _print_count,
  attrs = {
    "rule_dep": attr.label()
  }
)
```

Now, of course, we still need to invoke them via targets:

```
load("//:bazel/count_items.bzl", "count_items")
load("//:bazel/print_count.bzl", "print_count")

count_items(
    name="count",
    items=[1, 7, 13, 33],
)

print_count(
    name="print",
    rule_dep=":count",
)
```

And simply call the build:

```
bazel build print
```

This yields:

```
Loading:
Loading: 0 packages loaded
Analyzing: target //:print (0 packages loaded, 0 targets
configured)
DEBUG: /home/raptor/learn/projects/bazel-
book/code/rule_provider/bazel/print_count.bzl:5:3:
struct(count = 4) ①
DEBUG: /home/raptor/learn/projects/bazel-
book/code/rule_provider/bazel/print_count.bzl:8:3: Count
is 4
INFO: Analyzed target //:print (0 packages loaded, 0
targets configured).
INFO: Found 1 target...
[0 / 1] [Prepa] BazelWorkspaceStatusAction stable-
status.txt
Target //:print up-to-date (nothing to build) ②
INFO: Elapsed time: 0.097s, Critical Path: 0.01s
INFO: 0 processes.
INFO: Build completed successfully, 1 total action
INFO: Build completed successfully, 1 total action
```

① Our values are printed just fine.

② Since there is no `DefaultInfo`, there are no files, and no actions to be performed.

We ran through loading, then analysis, Bazel has seen there's nothing to do in the execution phase, so it just exits.

Beside the `DefaultInfo`, one last provider that I do want to mention is the `OutputGroupInfo` (https://docs.bazel.build/

versions/3.1.0/skylark/lib/OutputGroupInfo.html). We could output sets of files:

```
return [DefaultInfo(files = depset([binary])),
        OutputGroupInfo(debug_files =
depset([debug_file]),
                        optimized_files =
depset([optimized_file]))]
```

With a bunch of connection hidden (from the headers, and flags to each action) here's our graph, with each source file generating three outputs:

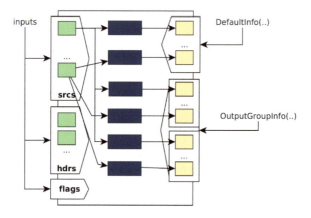

This approach also has command line support, allowing the picking of the target groups, by using the `--output_groups` argument [https://docs.bazel.build/versions/master/command-line-reference.html]. We could select a group by having `--output_groups=debug_files` when invoking the build.

## 2.2.4. Archiving Rule

Ok, let's go back to our *compile*, *link* and *archive* rules, we set out to implement at the beginning of this chapter.

We will start simple, with the archiving rule, since that's the easiest. All it needs is the input files and an output file that's resolved from the target name itself.

But since there is always a *name* parameter that identifies the target, we'll leverage that one, instead of adding an extra parameter to the rule. This parameter is accessible in the rule context as `ctx.label`.

```
def _archive(ctx):    ①
  out = ctx.actions.declare_file(ctx.label.name)
  args = ctx.actions.args()

  args.add(out)
  args.add_all(ctx.files.files)    ⑤

  ctx.actions.run(
    executable="zip",
    arguments=[args],
    inputs=ctx.files.files,
    outputs=[out])

  return [DefaultInfo(files=depset([out]))]

archive = rule(    ②
  implementation = _archive,
  attrs = {    ③
    "files": attr.label_list(allow_files=True),    ④
  }
)
```

Let's look now in more detail at the rule implementation, the
`_archive` function:

```python
def _archive(ctx):
    out = ctx.actions.declare_file(ctx.label.name)
    args = ctx.actions.args()

    args.add(out)
    args.add_all(ctx.files.files)

    ctx.actions.run(
        executable="zip",        ①
        arguments=[args],        ②
        inputs=ctx.files.files,  ③
        outputs=[out])           ④

    return [DefaultInfo(files=depset([out]))]
```

Let's break it down. First, we have the declaration of the output file that we will generate. Just declaring a file means we're getting a `File` object we can use in the code:

```python
out = ctx.actions.declare_file(ctx.label.name)
```

We still need to have an action that produces it.

This is simply a placeholder. It identifies an output of some action that our rule will generate later. We *must* define an action, and only one, that will output this file. In our case, we have the execution of a program, in this case, `zip`, that will write this file out:

```
ctx.actions.run(
  executable="zip",   ①
  arguments=[args],   ②
  inputs=ctx.files.files,   ③
  outputs=[out])   ④
```

① The program to execute.

② The arguments to the zip command.

③ *The input dependencies of the action node in the graph.* If these are missing, the files will not be copied to the sandbox folder.

④ The *output* files that this action will produce. These files can be chained to other actions.

This file is not in the output of the rule until we declare it as such:

```
return [DefaultInfo(files=depset([out]))]
```

# 2.2.5. Compilation Rule

The compilation rule code, while it still has the same structure with its declaration and implementation, unfortunately, is quite a bit more involved.

```
def _compile(ctx):
  output = []

  for f in ctx.files.srcs:
```

```
        out = ctx.actions.declare_file(
            "{}.o".format(f.path[:-2]))
        print("compiling {} -> {}".format(f, out))

        inputs = [f]
        inputs.extend(ctx.files.hdrs)

        args = ctx.actions.args()
        args.add(f)
        args.add("-o")
        args.add(out)

        args.add("-c")
        args.add("-I/usr/lib/gcc/x86_64-linux-gnu/7/include")

        output.append(out)

        ctx.actions.run(executable="gcc",
                        arguments=[args],
                        inputs=inputs,
                        outputs=[out])

    return [DefaultInfo(files=depset(output))]

compile = rule( ②
  implementation = _compile,   ③
  attrs = {  ③
    "srcs": attr.label_list(   ④
      allow_files=True,
      mandatory=True,
      allow_empty=False,
    ),
    "hdrs": attr.label_list(allow_files=True),
    "flags": attr.string(),
  }
)
```

There are a few things that you might have observed.

First, like we already discussed, we're going to leverage the Bazel graph. We are using the loop to construct the actions, by iterating using `for` over each input file we got in our `srcs` attribute:

```
for f in ctx.files.srcs:
  out = ctx.actions.declare_file(
      "{}.o".format(f.path[:-2]))
```

We're creating one output for each input source file. Later for that output, we define the action that will generate that file, using `ctx.actions.run(..)`:

```
ctx.actions.run(executable="gcc",
                arguments=[args],
                inputs=inputs,
                outputs=[out])
```

This code should be familiar from the `archive` rule we defined previously.

 Leverage the graph building of Bazel for better caching and faster builds.

The passing of some strange arguments into the `gcc` command we'll address later in *Native Rules*.

```
args.add("-c")
args.add("-I/usr/lib/gcc/x86_64-linux-gnu/7/include")
```

# 2.2.6. Linking Rule

Finally, the linking rule is just calling the linker:

```
def _link(ctx):
  out = ctx.actions.declare_file(ctx.attr.out)

  args = ctx.actions.args()
  args.add_all(ctx.files.objs)

  args.add("-o")
  args.add(out)
  args.add("-B")
  args.add("/usr/lib/gcc/x86_64-linux-gnu/7")
  args.add("-B")
  args.add("/usr/bin")

  ctx.actions.run(executable="/usr/bin/gcc",
                  arguments=[args],
                  inputs=ctx.files.objs,
                  outputs=[out])

  return [DefaultInfo(files=depset([out]))]

link = rule(
  implementation = _link,
  attrs = {
    "objs": attr.label_list(
      allow_files=True,
      mandatory=True,
      allow_empty=False,
    ),
    "out": attr.string(),
  }
)
```

The only thing more interesting here is again, passing the flags.

# 2.3. Basic Bazel Summary

In this chapter, we've seen the absolute fundamentals of Bazel. We went over the *action-graph* since this is how Bazel structures what needs to be built. We also mentioned the Bazel lifecycle with its *load*, *analyze*, and *execution* phases.

After we delved into *rules* and *targets*, we learned that *rules* are the functions that assemble actions together, and are the puzzle pieces Bazel uses to define our builds. We also have seen that *targets are in this context named invocations* of rules.

We then looked at actual samples, and we created three custom rules: archiving, compiling, and linking. We used them to see how rules are defined and implemented and how the action-graph gets chained.

Finally, we broke down the inputs and outputs for a rule, namely the *rule context*, the single God parameter that's the input, and the *providers* array that is the output.

# Chapter 3. Assembling Bazel Builds

# 3.1. Macros

We understand what a rule is now. We also see how we can chain them together using the outputs from the `DefaultInfo`. It also makes sense to have rules do a single simple thing: a compilation, an archival, a linking of a binary.

But what if we want to have a function that does all three, or sometimes only two steps? Or have it configurable? Here's where macros come into play.

Macros allow us to create something akin to a template over several rules, that creates multiple targets together. Macros are mere functions, but unlike the rules, they are just regular functions that a Python developer might expect. After macros execute, while all the rules invoked inside it leave traces via their created targets, the macro itself will cease to exist. It's the same as if the rules were independently called from the `BUILD` file one by one.

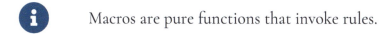 Macros are pure functions that invoke rules.

We will take the previous rules we defined during the last chapter:

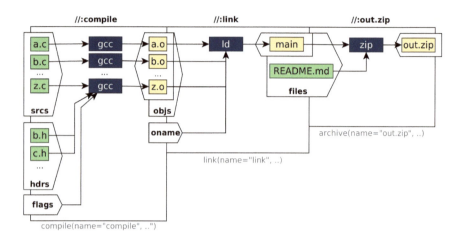

And wrap them in a macro. The macro function itself is incredibly simple:

```
load(":bazel/compile.bzl", "compile")
load(":bazel/link.bzl", "link")
load(":bazel/archive.bzl", "archive")

def application(name, srcs, hdrs, extra_files):   ①
    compile(   ②
      name="compile",
      srcs=srcs,
      hdrs=hdrs,
    )

    link(   ②
      name="link",
      objs=[":compile"],
      out="main",
    )

    archive_files = [":link"]
    archive_files.extend(extra_files)

    archive(   ②
      name=name,   ③
      files=archive_files,
    )
```

① Just a regular Skylark function.

② We're still invoking the rules like before.

③ We manually set the name of the rule from the `name`
   parameter of the macro.

If you noticed, we changed the archive, instead of having the
hardcoded target name, into reading the `name` parameter from
the macro. This `name` parameter is not required, but we do set it,
and we propagate the value to a rule, to have a target with the

same name, by convention.

We need it to make the target name explicit, so when we look at the `BUILD` file:

```
load(":bazel/application.bzl", "application")

application(
  name="main.zip",
  srcs=[
    "src/main.c",
    "src/print.c",
  ],
  hdrs=[
    "src/print.h",
  ],
  extra_files=[
    "src/README.md",
  ],
)
```

we immediately know we can call:

```
bazel build main.zip
```

Unfortunately, by just looking at the `load` statement, we can't tell if the thing we're bringing in the namespace is a rule or a macro. If it's a rule, when we instantiate it, we have a new target created. If it's a macro, we get whatever targets are defined in that macro function. If our macro would create some random target names, we wouldn't be able to know the target names by just checking the `BUILD` file. That's why we should be consistent and provide the `name` parameter always in macros.

 You should use a `name` parameter in your macro to make the target name explicit for the user.

 Macros invoke the rules but are not themselves part of the graph.

Now, if you noticed, the rules are having hardcoded names for `compile` and `link`, which defeats the purpose of having a reusable macro in the first place. If you'd try to run it twice, you'll get an error, since the same target name would be present multiple times, and as we established, a target name must be unique into a package. That's why let's rewrite the rule correctly:

```
load(":bazel/compile.bzl", "compile")
load(":bazel/link.bzl", "link")
load(":bazel/archive.bzl", "archive")

def application(name, srcs, hdrs, extra_files):
    compile_target_name = "{}-compile".format(name)   ①
    link_target_name = "{}-link".format(name)

    compile(
      name=compile_target_name,
      srcs=srcs,
      hdrs=hdrs,
    )

    link(
      name=link_target_name,
      objs=[compile_target_name],
      out="main",
    )

    archive_files = [link_target_name]
    archive_files.extend(extra_files)

    archive(
      name=name,   ②
      files=archive_files,
    )
```

① We generate the name of the dependent rules, using the given name.

② We propagate the name we got in the macro to the "main" target.

Now we can even invoke the same macro multiple times, and each invocation will invoke the three rule calls, creating different targets.

Since macros are untyped, it also means the variables for it are untyped. Regardless, whenever a rule is invoked, the parameters will be type-checked against the rule definition.

# 3.2. Native Rules

## 3.2.1. Genrule

Now that we understand rules and macros, we can address another critical topic: rules code size.

As you notice, there is a lot of code written to implement a simple program execution. Of course, a lot of this has to do with the way Bazel links files on actions. There's a bunch of boilerplate code. You might think it's a better idea to create a specific rule or macro that will stitch things together.

The good news is that this rule already exists, and is named, as you might have realized from the title of this section `genrule`. With it, we can create targets directly. Let's rewrite one of the archiving targets we did before using genrule, this time with it:

```
genrule(
  name="documentation",
  srcs=[
    "src/README.md",
  ],
  outs=[
      "documentation.zip",
  ],
  cmd="zip $(OUTS) $(SRCS)"
)
```

You might notice that there is no `load` statement for this rule. So, where does it come from? Bazel has a bunch of prepackaged rules targeted at various builds. These belong in the `native` package, and all the rule definitions are already visible as global rules into our `BAZEL` files.

Now we don't load any Bazel rule library but invoke one of the embedded rules of Bazel to create the targets. This `genrule` call has the drawback of leaking the implementation details - in this case, the `zip` command. But let's see what happens if we move it inside a macro:

```
def archive(name, files, out):
    native.genrule(  ①
        name=name,
        outs=[out],
        srcs=files,
        cmd="zip $(OUTS) $(SRCS)")
```

① The `native` module isn't implicitly imported in libraries, unlike the `BUILD` or `WORKSPACE` files. You need to use `native.genrule` , not just `genrule` .

Wow! This code is so much shorter!

Compare it with the rule implementation we did initially:

```
def _archive(ctx):   ①
    out_file = ctx.actions.declare_file(ctx.attr.out)
    args = ctx.actions.args()

    args.add(out_file)
    args.add_all(ctx.files.files)   ⑤

    ctx.actions.run(
        executable="zip",
        arguments=[args],
        inputs=ctx.files.files,
        outputs=[out_file])

    return [DefaultInfo(files=depset([out_file]))]   ⑥

archive = rule(   ②
    implementation = _archive,
    attrs = {   ③
        "files": attr.label_list(allow_files=True),   ④
        "out": attr.string(mandatory=True),
    }
)
```

And the real cool stuff is that we still have the same signature as before.

 We can use `genrule` to create targets if all they do is calling a short script.

Unlike `genrule`, actual rules could have multiple actions chained together. Simple rules are shown in debug graphs distinctively.

The last thing I want to touch on this topic is that the text inside the `cmd` attribute is a template. This is why we have `$(OUTS)` and `$(SRCS)` in there, that will get expanded to the actual file names that are used. Particularly this could be a problem when escaping characters since the `$(..)` means "execute the program and get its output" in UNIX shell scripting.

 Pay attention to `$(..)` when using genrules.

For straightforward command invocations, it might still pay off to use genrules.

## 3.2.2. Native Rules

The `native` package doesn't only contain `genrule`. In the `native` package, there's a lot of pre-written rules that support most of the build scenarios you'll encounter. If we'd list the `native` package, using `print(dir(native))` you'll see there's quite the mixture:

```
DEBUG: /home/raptor/learn/projects/bazel-
book/code/rule_debug/bazel/debug.bzl:3:3: ["aar_import",
"action_listener", "alias", "android_binary",
"android_device", "android_device_script_fixture",
"android_host_service_fixture",
"android_instrumentation_test", "android_library",
"android_local_test", "android_sdk",
"android_tools_defaults_jar", "apple_binary",
"apple_cc_toolchain", "apple_static_library",
"available_xcodes", "cc_binary",
"cc_host_toolchain_alias", "cc_import",
"cc_libc_top_alias", "cc_library", "cc_proto_library",
"cc_test", "cc_toolchain", "cc_toolchain_alias",
"cc_toolchain_suite", "config_feature_flag",
"config_setting", "constraint_setting",
"constraint_value", "environment", "existing_rule",
"existing_rules", "exports_files", "extra_action",
"fdo_prefetch_hints", "fdo_profile", "filegroup",
"genquery", "genrule", "glob", "j2objc_library",
"java_binary", "java_import", "java_library",
"java_lite_proto_library", "java_package_configuration",
"java_plugin", "java_proto_library", "java_runtime",
"java_runtime_alias", "java_test", "java_toolchain",
"java_toolchain_alias", "label_flag", "label_setting",
"ninja_build", "ninja_graph", "objc_import",
"objc_library", "package", "package_group",
"package_name", "platform", "proto_lang_toolchain",
"proto_library", "py_binary", "py_library", "py_runtime",
"py_test", "repository_name", "sh_binary", "sh_library",
"sh_test", "test_suite", "to_json", "to_proto",
"toolchain", "toolchain_type", "xcode_config",
"xcode_config_alias", "xcode_version"]
```

We have rules for building android applications, Java, Python, etc. If you wonder why let's go back to the rule we had to write for our C++ compilation, specifically this section:

```
args.add("-c")
args.add("-I/usr/lib/gcc/x86_64-linux-gnu/7/include")
```

We had to inject some magic flags manually, so our compilation would pass. We are quite limited in giving this kind of configuration from outside, without a significant amount of manual work.

This is the place where native rules shine. Native rules are implemented directly inside Bazel. Thus they can sidestep the limitation of running in the analysis phase and configure the actions correctly.

Don't forget, when executing Bazel code, we're running inside the Skylark environment, without access to the actual filesystem. The code we write is without side effects and only constructing the action graph. It's Bazel using this graph in the execution phase that will change the filesystem contents. That's not the case for the native rules, which allows them to do their magic.

Since native rules have this deep integration with the tools they support and don't require manual configuration, let's change our compiling/archiving project, and rely on the native `cc_binary` rule that allows us to compile C code:

```
load(":bazel/archive.bzl", "archive")

cc_binary(  ①
    name="main",
    srcs=[
        "src/main.c",
        "src/print.c",
        "src/print.h",
    ],
)

archive(
  name="out.zip",
  files=["src/README.md", ":main"],
)
```

① Both compilation and linking are done by `cc_binary`.

 A cool implementation detail: `cc_binary` also checks the headers included if they are declared as inputs.

Wow! Not only the code is significantly smaller, but also the magic of configuring the compiler is moved now onto Bazel's shoulders.

As we look at the comprehensive list of possible rules, we also understand that this list is most likely not sufficient. Sure, we should start here for basic things, but if you notice, what are our rules in the end? Just extra functions, written in Skylark, that we version together with the repository.

What if we could use shared libraries that allow us to add new rules and toolchains? So far, we have always used a single package and a single workspace. It's time to broaden our horizons about *packages and workspaces*, but before we do that, let's see a quick trick to get rid of manually listing files in rules.

# 3.2.3. Glob File Matching

As we already mentioned, we *must* specify all the files in the inputs of an action when we're creating that action. This quickly becomes a problem on any non-trivial project, since we would need to spell out all these references individually. Imagine having a Java project with 50 `.java` files that we manually write in our `BUILD` file. Fortunately, Bazel offers the `glob` function that we can use when assigning our parameters:

```
srcs = glob([
  "src/main/java/**/*.java"
]),
```

 `glob` gets resolved in the *loading* phase, not the *analysis*. That's why we cannot use `glob()` inside a rule implementation, but we can use it in macros.

The function call will expand as you can imagine to all the files that match the given pattern. `**` will match nested folders, including the current one, and `*` matches file name sections.

In our sample `src/main/java/**/*.java` matches all the `.java` files everywhere inside the `src/main/java/` folder. So if we added a new `.java` file, we wouldn't need to go and change the `BUILD` file again. For the rule itself, nothing changes. It would still get all the files as an expanded list, just like before, this time with the newly added file.

# 3.3. Packages and Workspaces

In Bazel, at the root of the whole project, is the definition of a workspace. Inside it, there can be one or more packages.

## 3.3.1. Workspace

The workspace of a project gets identified by a file named either `WORKSPACE`, or `WORKSPACE.bazel`, that contain references to external targets. External targets are various inputs we need for our actions to execute, be it other source code, dependencies, or tooling.

 The `WORKSPACE` file identifies the project's root and can define external targets.

There is a single `WORKSPACE` file that exists for the entire project, and that one defines the root of the project. All the packages reside inside folders below the folder containing the `WORKSPACE` folder, or in the same folder as the `WORKSPACE` file - as we had so far.

Now the external dependencies can be either other Bazel projects, some other non-Bazel projects, that we want to be built using Bazel, or just some common dependencies, such as libraries or tooling binaries.

# 3.3.2. Package

Inside the workspace, there can be one or more packages that define targets - rule invocations. A package is a folder that contains a file called `BUILD`, or `BUILD.bazel`. We've already seen them in the previous chapters, and now we know what they mean.

The `BUILD` file contains the target definitions - aka what can be built from this project. The relationship between them looks something like this:

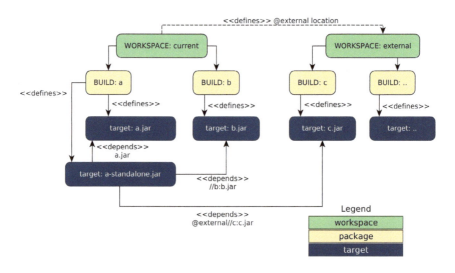

Think of a `BUILD` file similarly to a `pom.xml` if you come from the Java world, or `package.json` if you're a NodeJS person. It just defines how to assemble the artifact we want, starting from some inputs, and applying some reusable algorithms that process them - the rules we've seen so far.

  A `BUILD` file identifies a package.

Packages also exist to split the graph into more chewable components and to break down dependencies. They contain visibility rules, meaning we can't randomly get the targets from another package unless the package is exposing them.

A `BUILD` file identifies the root of the package. If, in another nested folder, there is another `BUILD` file, that following file defines the boundary of another package, and all the visibility rules apply.

Let's assume we have the following folder structure. Here the solid border defines a package boundary, while the dotted ones show regular folders. There is a one to one direct correspondence between package names, and the folder structures their `BUILD` files reside in:

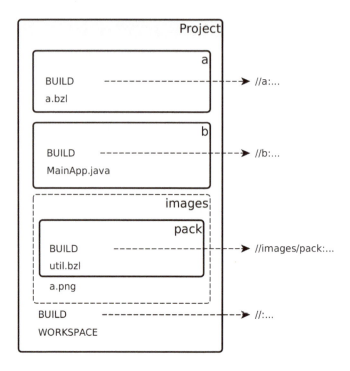

In the previous example, we can't access from the root package `//:` the `images/pack/util.bzl` directly, since it belongs to the `//images/pack:`. So to refer to it, for example in a `load` statement, we'd need to point to `//images/pack:util.bzl`, while `//:images/pack/util.bzl` would return an error.

Each `BUILD` file defines a package and creates its boundary, regardless of where in the subtree it belongs. To cross that boundary and refer to a target inside a package, we need to have permissions given via visibility modifiers.

Furthermore, remember the inputs and outputs of the rules? The package also limits where rules can write. Whenever we write files, we *must* write them inside the current package. Our rule actions cannot write anything outside the package from where the rule gets invoked.

# 3.3.3. Labels

It is an excellent time to introduce something we've already seen a few times, namely, how do we address targets or files, including across different packages, and even different workspaces. We use *labels* to reference resources across workspaces, packages, and files inside our packages.

 A label is a standardized naming convention to point to targets.

The format is rather simple:

```
@external-name//path/to/package:path/inside/package
```

|  Legend |
| --- |
| @ workspace identifier |
| // package identifier |
| : package/file separator |

A label is split into three sections.

The first part defines what workspace we're referring to. If it's present, it is prefixed with an `@` symbol. The actual mapping to the external workspace is into the `WORKSPACE` file. The label refers to targets in the current workspace if the path is empty (`//some/package:target`, i.e., no `@`).

Check the `WORKSPACE` file to find out external workspace mappings.

The second part of the label is the package's path, that's literally only a folder containing a `BUILD` file. There is a one-to-one mapping from the folder structure to the package names inside a workspace. The second part can also be missing, and then we could have only the last part.

The last part, after the `:` sign, is the target inside the package. If the package name before it is missing, so no `//` prefix, it means this label identifies a target in the current package.

If only the package path is present, i.e. `//some/folder`, then the target name is implied from the last folder path, so this is equivalent to `//some/folder:folder`. This substitution might look counter-intuitive, but remember, labels always point to targets.

 Labels always refer to targets.

So whenever you've seen:

```
bazel build archive
```

It was to build the target named *archive*, in the current package. Since, in our case, it was only the root package, that was the equivalent of `//:archive`.

Let's return to the *label* parameters we passed into our rules before, where we had the `allow_file`(s) . In the `ctx.attr` we would have the *label*, but in the `ctx.file`, or the `ctx.files` if this is a label list, we would have the *resolved file(s)*, from the targets.

For example in a *label attribute* called `srcs` that has `allow_files=True`, in the rule context we would find `ctx.attr.srcs` containing the *label* values, and the `ctx.files.srcs` contains the *expanded list of files outputted by the targets*.

So while the label list might be something such as `["//:documentation", "//:test.txt"]` in the rule attribute, and in the `ctx.attr` respectively, this could resolve to multiple files `["/../README.md", "/../README.adoc", "/../test.txt"]` in the `ctx.files` for the same attribute key.

# 3.3.4. External Workspaces

We covered a lot of ground, but we arrived at something new, by mentioning we could have external workspaces. External workspaces are what the name implies. They contain targets residing outside our current project. As you remember, we can have a single `WORKSPACE` file that defines our project's root, and this `WORKSPACE` file lists the external workspaces if any are present.

We use *external workspaces* to *refer to external targets* that, in turn, could bring new content into our build. These mean brand-new files as dependencies to our project or extra tooling used to assemble the project. Let's not forget that compilers and parsers at the end of the day, are just files, that can be built and become simple action inputs, so they could also be simply fetched from an external workspace.

 Whenever you hear external dependencies, immediately think WORKSPACE .

So as the last magnum opus, let's do just that. We'll create a rule written in Java that depends on Maven dependencies. This sample will illustrate everything: multiple packages with visibility settings, external dependencies, and a different programming language to implement actions instead of shell scripting, namely Java.

 Bazel needs Python to execute, so consider Python in easily creating cross-platform actions.

The rule that we'll implement is the archiving rule. We'll go with 7z as the algorithm (SevenZip) since it's not included in Java by default, so it allows us to fetch maven dependencies and illustrates external workspaces. Lastly, it has a significantly better compress rate than the stock zip algorithm's bundled in Java.

Bazel doesn't out of the box supports Maven. So we need to add support for it. You guessed it! To bring it in, we'll first load an external rule into our `WORKSPACE` file. Unsurprisingly, this external rule needs also fetching into the current workspace. So we first fetch the maven support, then using it we fetch the external maven dependencies.

To achieve this, we'll do:

```
load("@bazel_tools//tools/build_defs/repo:http.bzl",
"http_archive")  ①

RULES_JVM_EXTERNAL_TAG = "3.2"
RULES_JVM_EXTERNAL_SHA =
"82262ff4223c5fda6fb7ff8bd63db8131b51b413d26eb49e3131037e
79e324af"

http_archive(  ②
    name = "rules_jvm_external",
    strip_prefix = "rules_jvm_external-%s" %
RULES_JVM_EXTERNAL_TAG,
    sha256 = RULES_JVM_EXTERNAL_SHA,
    url =
"https://github.com/bazelbuild/rules_jvm_external/archive
/%s.zip" % RULES_JVM_EXTERNAL_TAG,
)

load("@rules_jvm_external//:defs.bzl", "maven_install")
③

maven_install(  ④
    artifacts = [
      "org.apache.commons:commons-compress:1.20",
      "commons-io:commons-io:2.7",
      "org.tukaani:xz:1.8",
    ],
    repositories = [
        "https://jcenter.bintray.com/",
        "https://maven.google.com",
        "https://repo1.maven.org/maven2",
    ],
)
```

① We start with loading a rule that already is part of Bazel, just not in the `native` package, the `http_archive` rule.

② Using `http_archive` we fetch the `maven_install` rule definition.

③ We load the `maven_install` into our context.

④ We invoke it and create the maven targets.

The `@bazel_tools` external workspace, despite looking like an external workspace *is bundled* in Bazel. This statement gives us the `http_archive` rule that fetches a remote Bazel archived project. You'll see that in the next rule that we'll download, the `maven_install` one.

> `@bazel_tools` contains multiple rules for fetching other projects, including creating projects from non-Bazel archives.

This new rule, the `http_archive` one, fetches a remote Bazel project archive and makes it available as an external workspace. The critical part is the name definition because that says what's the external workspace name that we'll use.

```
name = "rules_jvm_external",
```

Then we use the name of the target as the external workspace. This *rules_jvm_external* is the name of the external workspace as defined by the `http_archive` rule invocation. *Inside the remote archive, there is another Bazel project.* This workspace is a regular external workspace that we can use for our `load` statements.

So we'll load the `maven_install` rule, from the external

workspace:

```
load("@rules_jvm_external//:defs.bzl", "maven_install")
③
```

So finally we can use the rule, to download the actual maven artifacts:

```
maven_install(   ④
    artifacts = [
        "org.apache.commons:commons-compress:1.20",
        "commons-io:commons-io:2.7",
        "org.tukaani:xz:1.8",
    ],
    repositories = [
        "https://jcenter.bintray.com/",
        "https://maven.google.com",
        "https://repo1.maven.org/maven2",
    ],
)
```

This creates another external workspace named `@maven`. We can still use the `name` attribute and create different external workspaces. This attribute becomes especially important since the `maven_install` rule generates the name of the target only from the *groupId*, and the *artifactId* of the maven GAV id. This rule will create a target called `@maven//org_apache_commons_commons_compress`, ignoring the version.

In case you don't know Maven, GAV identifies artifacts, i.e. jar files, and stands for *groupId*, *archiveId*, and *version*. You can see in

this example we have an artifact named:
`org.apache.commons:commons-compress:1.20`. It means its
*groupId* is `org.apache.commons`, the *artifactId* is `commons-compress`, and it's on version `1.20`.

Maven uses this as a hierarchical structure to declare packages,
allowing different organizations to publish artifacts with the
same *artifactId*, without risk of collision, since they would be
under different groups. This is significantly different from *npm*
or *pypi*, where all the packages are in a flat list.

Because of this limitation of the `maven_install` rule, we can't
have the same artifact in two versions in the same target. So if
we would need a different version of the same artifact (same
groupId, and same artifactId), we would just create another
target `maven_install(name="maven1", ..)` and refer to the
artifact in the different version: `@maven1//..`.

Now, the next step is invoking the `java_binary` rule that creates
our Java program target:

```
java_binary(   ①
  name = "_seven_zip_binary",
  srcs = glob([
    "src/main/java/**/*.java"
  ]),
  main_class = "com.germaniumhq.ArchiveRule",   ②
  deps = [
    "@maven//:org_apache_commons_commons_compress",   ③
    "@maven//:commons_io_commons_io",
    "@maven//:org_tukaani_xz",
  ]
)

package(default_visibility = ["//visibility:public"])   ④
```

① We're using the `java_binary` native rule

② We say what's the main class

③ We point to the maven dependencies

④ We make all the targets in this package public

The `java_binary` rule does multiple things. It compiles the code and makes a script available, which can be used as an executable in actions. We can use this target later in our `seven_zip` rule definition:

```
seven_zip = rule(
  implementation = _seven_zip,
  attrs = {
    "_seven_zip_binary": attr.label(
        executable=True,    ①
        default=":_seven_zip_binary",    ②
        cfg="host",    ③
    ),
    "version_data": attr.label(    ④
        allow_single_file=True,
        mandatory=True,
    ),
    "archive_files": attr.label_list(    ⑤
        allow_files=True,
        mandatory=True,
        allow_empty=False
    ),
  }
)
```

① This label is special, since it points to an executable

② The target name is the one we defined in the `java_binary` rule invocation.

③ Executables must specify the `cfg` attribute. This can be either `"host"` if the executable is part of the build - i.e. a compiler, or `"target"` if the executable is part of the later runtime, i.e. testing.

④ To make the rule more interesting, beside archiving multiple files we're also creating another synthetic file from the *content* of another. This approach is attractive in scenarios such as ingesting *external data*.

⑤ This is the list of files that we'll add to the archive.

Implementing this rule in Skylark is very straightforward; we're merely invoking the program with the arguments:

```python
def _seven_zip(ctx):
  out = ctx.actions.declare_file(
"{}.7z".format(ctx.label.name))   ①

    inputs = [ ctx.file.version_data ]   ②
    inputs.extend(ctx.files.archive_files)   ③

    args = ctx.actions.args()
    args.add(out)   ①
    args.add(ctx.file.version_data)   ②
    args.add_all(ctx.files.archive_files)   ③

    ctx.actions.run(
      executable=ctx.executable._seven_zip_binary,   ④
      arguments=[args],
      inputs=inputs,
      outputs=[out])

    return [DefaultInfo(files=depset([out]))]
```

① We're declaring the output file and passing the name as an argument to the Java program

② We send the `version_data` name, to be read by the main program. Note that we need it as an input for our action as well, so it's part of the action graph. Otherwise, we'll see it as an argument when the program runs, but get a *file not found* exception later since the file itself isn't copied into the sandbox.

③ We pass the names of all the files using `add_all` this time, instead of `add`

④ We're adding our action in the graph pointing to the Java
program launcher script as the executable

Now the actual Java program itself is not super spectacular, but
we'll show it anyway. The only thing that it's worth noticing it
that *we must write the outputs* as part of our execution. Of course,
this is similar to what we had before in our rules; it is just that
this time we do it in Java code. Actions need to write output
files:

```java
public static void main(String[] args) throws IOException
{
    Deque<String> parameters = new
ArrayDeque<>(Arrays.asList(args));   ①
    String outputFileName = readString(parameters);
    String commitVersion = readFileContent(parameters);
    List<String> inputFiles = new
ArrayList<>(parameters);

    File outputFile = new File(outputFileName);

    try (SevenZOutputStream out = new SevenZOutputStream(
            new SevenZOutputFile(outputFile))) {   ②
        File commitInformation = new File("commit-
info.txt");   ③
        SevenZArchiveEntry commitInfoEntry =
out.getOutputFile().createArchiveEntry(
            commitInformation,
commitInformation.getName());

out.getOutputFile().putArchiveEntry(commitInfoEntry);

        IOUtils.write(String.format("Version: %s",
commitVersion), out, "utf-8");
```

```
                out.getOutputFile().closeArchiveEntry();

            for (String fileName: inputFiles) {   ④
                File file = new File(fileName);
                SevenZArchiveEntry entry =
    out.getOutputFile().createArchiveEntry(
                        file, file.getName());
                out.getOutputFile().putArchiveEntry(entry);

                try (InputStream fis = new
    FileInputStream(file)) {
                    IOUtils.copy(fis, out);
                }

                out.getOutputFile().closeArchiveEntry();
            }
        }
    }
```

① We parse the input arguments.

② We create the 7z output.

③ We write our `commit-info.txt` with the content from the
version file. This is just a sample to show we can do any kind
of extra processing.

④ We add all the other input files

The reading of the parameters is also abstracted:

```
private static String readString(Deque<String>
parameters) {
    return parameters.poll();
}
```

And since we will read many parameters as outputs from other rules, we'll have another function that reads them directly as content.

```
private static String readFileContent(Deque<String>
parameters) throws IOException {
    if (parameters.isEmpty()) {
        throw new IllegalArgumentException("Unable to
read parameters.");
    }

    try (InputStream is = new
FileInputStream(parameters.poll())) {
        return IOUtils.toString(is,
StandardCharsets.UTF_8);
    }
}
```

Now using this rule still happens just as before in our `BUILD` file:

```
load("//bazel/archive:seven_zip.bzl", "seven_zip")

seven_zip(
  name="data",
  version_data="//version:data.txt",
  archive_files=[
    "users.txt",
    "groups.txt",
  ]
)
```

It's just that since the executable for the action is a target itself, it just becomes part of the graph. So now, as part of the build, the SevenZip archiver will be compiled first. Then using the newly built tool, the archiving will be performed.

Now, maybe the SevenZip example looks boring. Imagine that instead of it, there was a custom build process you'd need to apply. You can plug in custom Java code *as part of the build itself*, and have it versioned with the repository.

# 3.3.5. Repository Rules

We've seen now the `maven_install` being fetched from remote. Which raises the question, what *is* this? You probably guessed it from the `load` statement, and the invocation with the `name` attribute that this is a rule.

Now, this rule is not a regular `rule`, but a `repository_rule`. It still has a context - this time, a repository context [https://docs.bazel.build/versions/master/skylark/lib/repository_ctx.html], and generates *full Bazel workspaces*. Yes, that means creating folders that can hold multiple packages, ensuring all the `BUILD` files with their target definitions, and any other extra source files needed exist.

Of course, this generation of the full Bazel workspace could be a simple download of an archive containing all these files, not necessarily creating them from scratch. This download is what `http_archive` does here - simply downloads it and unpacks it. That's why when we see:

```
http_archive(  ②
    name = "rules_jvm_external",
    strip_prefix = "rules_jvm_external-%s" %
RULES_JVM_EXTERNAL_TAG,
    sha256 = RULES_JVM_EXTERNAL_SHA,
    url =
"https://github.com/bazelbuild/rules_jvm_external/archive
/%s.zip" % RULES_JVM_EXTERNAL_TAG,
)

load("@rules_jvm_external//:defs.bzl", "maven_install")
③
```

Looking at the load statement, it's clear now that there is a `BUILD` file in the root of that archive defining a package at the root of the workspace. This is why the target definition `@rules_jvm_external//:defs.bzl` works. If we breakdown this target name, we can see:

- `@rules_jvm_external` - external workspace, defined in the `WORKSPACE` file, with a `repository_rule` invocation.
- `//:` - package inside the workspace. In this case, root.
- `defs.bzl` - target inside the package. Here, an exported file.

Since we're running in the Workspace context, the `name` attribute in the repository rule invocation is not a target anymore, but rather it defines the external workspace name.

To further solidify this knowledge, we'll write our own repository rule that enables us to download remote files. While this repository rule we'll write just downloads files, since we can execute programs and generate data in repository rules, the sky's the limit on what we can do.

So in our rule, we want to point to remote URLs and automatically have targets created for them. The usage in the WORKSPACE will look like this:

```
load("//:bazel/download_url.bzl", "download_url")

download_url(
  name="index-germanium",
  url="http://germaniumhq.com/",
)

download_url(
  name="index-google",
  url="https://google.com/",
)
```

To keep things simple on the usage side, we'll create a target called data in a root package, in the generated external workspace. That's why when referring to the targets, we'll use only //:data against the external workspace in the BUILD file:

```
genrule(
  name="indexes",
  srcs=[
    "@index-germanium//:data",
    "@index-google//:data",
  ],
  outs=[
      "out.zip",
  ],
  cmd="zip $(OUTS) $(SRCS)"
)
```

The actual code of the rule implementation has a lot of the
familiar feeling:

```
def _download_url(repoctx):   ①
  # repoctx has `download` bundled in for downloading,
  # we're using `execute` to show generation can happen
in any
  # form
  repoctx.report_progress("downloading: " +
repoctx.attr.url)   ②

  repoctx.file(   ③
    "BUILD",
    content='exports_files(["data"])',
    executable=False)

  exec_result = repoctx.execute([   ④
    "curl", "-o", "data", repoctx.attr.url
  ])

  if exec_result.return_code != 0:
    fail("Unable to download {url}\nOUT: {stdout}\nERR:
{stderr}".format(
      url=repoctx.attr.url,
      stdout=exec_result.stdout,
      stderr=exec_result.stderr,
    ))

download_url = repository_rule(   ①
  implementation = _download_url,
  attrs = {
    "url": attr.string(mandatory=True),
  }
)
```

① Is a regular function, wired through `repository_rule`, with
   its implementation bound via the *implementation* attribute.
   The attributes are still there like before. The rule has a single
   parameter, this time a *repository context*, with a different API

[https://docs.bazel.build/versions/master/skylark/lib/repository_ctx.html] than the *rule context*.

② We can report to the user what's happening. These messages will appear when running the build as the description of the active task.

③ We're writing a new file. *Unlike the regular rules, in repository rules, the file gets immediately written.* We also see the declaration of another package, via writing the `BUILD` file, with a single target that will get exposed, named `data`.

④ The file `data` will be downloaded. Again, unlike regular rules, this time, *the execution happens immediately.*

So if we look back at one of its invocations ( `WORKSPACE` ):

```
download_url(
  name="index-germanium",
  url="http://germaniumhq.com/",
)
```

And at the reference of its target from the external repository ( `BUILD` ):

```
genrule(
  name="indexes",
  srcs=[
    "@index-germanium//:data",
    "@index-google//:data",
  ],
  outs=[
      "out.zip",
  ],
  cmd="zip $(OUTS) $(SRCS)"
)
```

Then I hope it all makes sense now, and there is no more "magic" still going on. We're merely referring to the external workspace, hence the @ symbol, and try to get one of its targets.

 When the external workspace targets get referred, Bazel executes *all its commands defined in the workspace.*

Now the previous note is sort of obvious since we're not stitching actions anymore in a graph, but instead, immediately write files or invoke programs.

Another thing worth mentioning is that even if targets are in external workspaces, the same rules of creating the action-graph, analyzing it, and invoking only the relevant actions required for the requested targets' output apply. While in this case, the external workspace was defining a static file as a target and export it via `exports_files(["data"])`, we could also have targets that are the result of multiple steps applied in the graph, in the like of what we discussed in the *Rules and Targets*.

This graph with target dependencies is what makes in my opinion Bazel great for builds. We could switch out full subgraphs, and as long as the targets still get generated, our build will always be fine.

# 3.3.6. BAZEL, WORKSPACE, and Regular bzl files

Okay, so we've seen quite a lot of code, and we established that this code written in Skylark is a lot like Python. Skylark tries a lot to have the same syntax and types as Python. You'll see all the collections and the APIs try to emulate Python as close as possible. `format` and `%` string interpolations, list comprehensions, `set`, `dict`, `list`, you name it, they're there.

Unlike Python, in Skylark `dict` and `set` keep the ordering of insertion when iterating over the elements. This is great for adding command-line arguments or other items in actions.

Now, of course, all other constructs are also present, such as creating functions using `def`, iterating over items using `for`, or `if` statements.

You might find it strange, but no `try`/`except` is available. As we understand now that rules don't invoke commands, but instead, just stitch the graph together, we can live without them. If we need to fail the build, we can do it by calling `fail` inside a rule. Even in repository rules, where running programs happen instantaneously, a command execution itself will return an error code that can be checked, so an exception can only appear if there's a bug in the rule construction code.

Another thing that's worth mentioning is that it is not possible to define functions, nor use code control statements inside the `BAZEL` and `WORKSPACE` files. The reason for that is that both the package definition and the project definition files are meant to declare targets.

It's still possible to declare constants or use list comprehensions. As we've seen already, it's also possible to `load` a macro or a function from another file and invoke it. But the `WORKSPACE` and `BUILD` files are there only to declare the targets available. This is why my recommendation is in macros to always create a target with the same `name` attribute passed in the macro.

Because when we look inside the `WORKSPACE` or `BUILD` files, we should immediately see what's possible to build out of these packages or what external workspaces are defined.

# 3.4. External Data

We covered quite a bit of ground so far in building our source code. We even have introduced custom tooling as part of the build itself. Unfortunately, we still have a smaller elephant in the room. How do we get external data into our build?

If you remember, we discussed right at the beginning that Bazel starts with an empty sandbox for content and files that we want to access into our build, we need to have them as inputs to our actions, so they get copied into the sandbox.

So imagine we want to access the git commit hash somehow. If we run `git rev-parse HEAD` into an action, we'll get an error, because there is no git repository in our sandbox. We could go and define as a dependency to our action on all git files - `glob("//:.git/**/*")` - but that's way too extreme.

If we expose it into an environment variable and try to access it the program implementing the action, you'll notice that Bazel prunes the environment variables from your local shell, even standard ones such as `PATH` get rewritten. This environment cleanup is the reason why we needed to pass these flags into our compilation rule, or switch to the native `cc_binary` rule, as we've previously seen with *native rules*:

```
args.add("-c")
args.add("-I/usr/lib/gcc/x86_64-linux-gnu/7/include")
```

We'll look at two ways Bazel allows us to get data inside our builds: via environment variables, then via running an external program that populates two files.

# 3.4.1. Environment Variables

Environment variables are necessary for many reasons. They're rather intuitive and easy to debug, only a `set` away into finding the local system's values when developing. They also provide a way to get values in without having files written - subject to Bazel caching, particularly useful for credentials where we don't want them to touch the disk.

To inject environment variables, we need a few hoops, but it's surprisingly straightforward to implement. On the one hand, we need to specify that our rule needs the environment variables injected. On the other hand, we need to instruct Bazel into what variables we are interested in reading from the current environment.

So let's define an environment variable:

```
export MY_JDBC_URL="jdbc:postgresql://localhost/test"
```

Now, we'll define a rule that uses it:

```
def _write_jdbc(ctx):
  out = ctx.actions.declare_file(
"{}.cfg".format(ctx.label.name))

  args = ctx.actions.args()
  args.add(out)

  ctx.actions.run_shell(
    command="""
      echo "JDBC is $MY_JDBC_URL"
      echo "$MY_JDBC_URL" > $1
    """,
    use_default_shell_env=True,   ①
    arguments=[args],
    outputs=[out])

  return [DefaultInfo(files=depset([out]))]

write_jdbc = rule(
  implementation = _write_jdbc,
)
```

① Note the use of the `use_default_shell_env=True`. Without this flag, the variable won't be accessible to our action. We need to enable it for our action explicitly. This is the first part of getting the variables in: telling Bazel this action requires the environment variables injected.

Let's define a small package `BUILD` file:

```
load("//:bazel/write_jdbc.bzl", "write_jdbc")

write_jdbc(name="db")
```

We might be tempted just to run the build for it:

```
bazel build db
```

However, when we do that we're in for a surprise:

```
Loading:
Loading: 0 packages loaded
Analyzing: target //:db (1 packages loaded, 0 targets
configured)
INFO: Analyzed target //:db (4 packages loaded, 6 targets
configured).
INFO: Found 1 target...
[0 / 2] [Prepa] BazelWorkspaceStatusAction stable-
status.txt
INFO: From Action db.cfg:
JDBC is   ①
Target //:db up-to-date:
  bazel-bin/db.cfg
INFO: Elapsed time: 0.506s, Critical Path: 0.05s
INFO: 1 process: 1 linux-sandbox.
INFO: Build completed successfully, 2 total actions
INFO: Build completed successfully, 2 total actions
```

① The variable is *empty*.

The reason for that is that not all environment variables are automatically read. It wouldn't even make sense to read the whole user environment since it could have drastic effects on the execution. This is the second step of getting the environment variables in. We need to add them manually one by one into the Bazel context at runtime:

```
bazel build db --action_env=MY_JDBC_URL
```

If we would have multiple parameters, we'd need several `--action_env` set. Then we get what we expect:

```
Loading:
Loading: 0 packages loaded
Analyzing: target //:db (0 packages loaded, 0 targets
configured)
INFO: Analyzed target //:db (0 packages loaded, 0 targets
configured).
INFO: Found 1 target...
[0 / 2] [Prepa] Action db.cfg
INFO: From Action db.cfg:
JDBC is jdbc:postgresql://localhost/test   ①
Target //:db up-to-date:
  bazel-bin/db.cfg
INFO: Elapsed time: 0.389s, Critical Path: 0.07s
INFO: 1 process: 1 linux-sandbox.
INFO: Build completed successfully, 2 total actions
INFO: Build completed successfully, 2 total actions
```

① The variable is correctly read.

 You need to add *both* `use_default_shell_env=True` to the rule, and pass the `--action_env` flag into the `bazel` `build` command to get the environment variables propagated.

Furthermore, if we change the environment variable:

```
export MY_JDBC_URL=jdbc:postgresql://localhost/test-prod
```

And run the build:

```
bazel build db --action_env=MY_JDBC_URL
```

We'll see that the action executes again:

```
Loading:
Loading: 0 packages loaded
Analyzing: target //:db (0 packages loaded, 0 targets
configured)
INFO: Analyzed target //:db (0 packages loaded, 0 targets
configured).
INFO: Found 1 target...
[0 / 1] [Prepa] BazelWorkspaceStatusAction stable-
status.txt
INFO: From Action db.cfg:
JDBC is jdbc:postgresql://localhost/test-prod  ①
Target //:db up-to-date:
  bazel-bin/db.cfg
INFO: Elapsed time: 0.145s, Critical Path: 0.06s
INFO: 1 process: 1 linux-sandbox.
INFO: Build completed successfully, 2 total actions
INFO: Build completed successfully, 2 total actions
```

① value is updated.

That's because environment variables are also part of the caching. Of course, it gets tedious to pass all these in every command. You can create a `.bazelrc` file to specify automatically flags to be set:

```
build --action_env=MY_JDBC_URL
```

Then there's no need to add the flags on each execution manually.

 Use `.bazelrc` to add the environment flags.

## 3.4.2. Workspace Status Command

`bazel build` has an argument named `--workspace_status_command` that will run *outside the sandbox*, and *before the actual build*.

We can point it to a program or a script, and this program will get started by Bazel, and its output captured. Each line the script outputs is considered a variable. The name of the variable is the text up to the first space. If the line doesn't contain a space, it's dropped. Bazel writes the variables in two files, depending on the variable type.

 For reasons unknown, the script cannot be in the Workspace's root, but must be in a folder.

There are two kinds of variables in the status command: *stable* and *volatile*:

- *Stable* ones have the name beginning with `STABLE_` and get written into the `stable-status.txt`. This file is a regular file available as an `input` for an action using the `ctx.info_file` field, from the action context.

- *Volatile* variables are all the other variables, and get persisted into the `volatile-status.txt`. This additional file is also available for input in actions, from the `ctx.version_file` of the action context.

 The `STABLE_` prefix marks *stable* variables. Any other is a *volatile* variable.

The difference between them is that *volatile* variables are for variables that often change, and *do not invalidate the cache*. That's why whenever values change for the `volatile-status.txt` variables, the downstream actions that have it as an input won't get the cache invalidated, and won't get executed again if the only change is a volatile variable.

 Changes in the `volatile-status.txt` (`ctx.version_file`) do not invalidate caches for actions that depend on it.

It doesn't sound straightforward, but it's easier than it seems. Let's imagine we have this simple shell script:

```
#!/bin/bash

echo "CURRENT_TIME $(date -Iseconds)"
echo "STABLE_GIT_COMMIT
9857f3a44de9a3c0869205733b1f2b6942eb50df"
echo "STABLE_VERSION 1"
echo "HOSTNAME germanium"
echo "CURRENT_IP 123.1.1.1"
```

Of course, in reality, the script will do more than merely echoing static values. Since this is a script, we can execute anything that we want. We could run commands such as `git rev-parse HEAD` since we are running *outside* the actual build, and *inside* our current source tree. This script could even be something else than a shell script such as Python.

So this is how Bazel will fan out the variables in files, after the calling of the script:

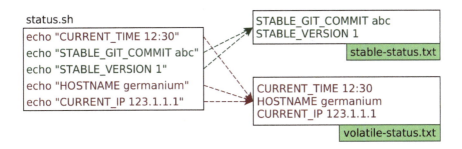

Now let's assume we want a rule that uses the value of `STABLE_GIT_COMMIT` and `CURRENT_TIME` writing them into a file. Let's say we want to say when our project was last build, with what git commit version. We'll start with a naive approach, then delve into how to do it better.

Let's start simple in `bazel/status.bzl`:

```python
def _status(ctx):
  # WRONG! DON'T IMPLEMENT LIKE THIS.
  out = ctx.actions.declare_file(ctx.label.name)

  args = ctx.actions.args()
  args.add(ctx.info_file)      ①
  args.add(ctx.version_file)   ②
  args.add(out)                ③

  ctx.actions.run_shell(
    command=""" ④
      echo "Project Status $(cat $1 | grep GIT | cut -f2
-d\ ) built at $(cat $2 | grep CURRENT_TIME | cut -f2 -d\
)." > $3
    """,
    arguments=[args],
    inputs=[ctx.version_file, ctx.info_file],   ⑤
    outputs=[out])

  return [DefaultInfo(files=depset([out]))]

status = rule(
  implementation = _status,
)
```

① The *stable* variables file, is obtained from the `ctx.info_file`.

② The *volatile* variables file, is obtained from the `ctx.version_file`.

③ This is just the regular output.

④ We read the variables from the files, so we need to grep them out.

⑤ We add the files as regular dependencies.

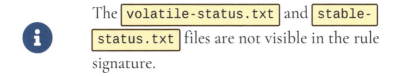 The `volatile-status.txt` and `stable-status.txt` files are not visible in the rule signature.

This is how the whole things look like:

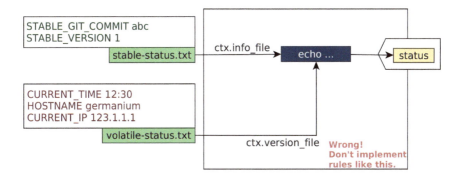

If we run it:

```
bazel build --workspace_status_command=bazel/status.sh
```

We see it executes successfully, and the `bazel-bin/status` file written contains the correct output:

```
Project Status 9857f3a44de9a3c0869205733b1f2b6942eb50df
built at 2020-05-27T23:21:15+02:00.
```

Furthermore, if we rerun it, even if the date changed, our action won't get called, and the cached version is used instead. That's because our `CURRENT_TIME` always gets written in the volatile variables. If anything changes impacting `stable-status.txt`, on a rerun of `bazel build`, the date will also be adjusted accordingly.

And this shows the problem with this approach. If *anything* changes in the `stable-status.txt` the cache is invalidated. Of course, for our `echo` rule, it doesn't mean much. But if the rule were some complicated process, that would come to bite us hard. An enormous chunk of the downstream actions might get executed even if the stable variables we need for rule haven't changed. That's why we need to go back and take advantage of Bazel's graph.

# 3.4.3. Breaking Variables

Let's create a rule that extracts a single variable from the `stable-status.txt` and writes it into its a file containing precisely that one variable. The target created will have the same name as the variable, and we will create a distinct package for the variables. Something like this:

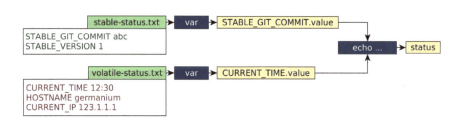

Why? Remember that caching in Bazel happens in the context

of the content, not timestamps. If our action writes some output, the content of that output file gets cached. But what happens if the action generates the same content again? The next action in the chain doesn't execute *at all*, and instead, the previously cached result it's used. This caching can potentially yield tremendous performance improvements.

 Use a rule that extracts individual variables from the `stable-status.txt` to leverage the Bazel graph.

So let's write this rule into a new file `vars/single_variable.bzl`:

```
def _single_variable(ctx):
  out = ctx.actions.declare_file(
"{}.value".format(ctx.label.name))   ①

    if ctx.label.name.startswith("STABLE_"):   ②
      input_file = ctx.info_file
    else:
      input_file = ctx.version_file

    args = ctx.actions.args()
    args.add(ctx.label.name)
    args.add(input_file)
    args.add(out)

    ctx.actions.run_shell(
      command="""
        grep "^$1 " $2 | sed -e "s/^$1 //" > $3
      """,
      arguments=[args],
      inputs=[input_file],   ③
      outputs=[out])

    return [DefaultInfo(files=depset([out]))]

  single_variable = rule(
    implementation = _single_variable,
  )
```

① We use the variable name in the filename we'll output.

② We also use the variable name to determine the input file for the variable that we're reading.

③ We use this input file as an input dependency for our action.

The extraction of each variable happens by creating targets. We do that into our new package designed especially for that

( `vars/BUILD` ):

```
load("//vars:single_variable.bzl", "single_variable")  ①

single_variable(name="STABLE_GIT_COMMIT")  ②
single_variable(name="CURRENT_TIME")

package(default_visibility = ["//visibility:public"])  ③
```

① We load our rule into the package context.

② To extract a variable, we call the `single_variable` rule, and the target name defines the variable to be extracted. Note that the action that builds the `//vars:STABLE_GIT_COMMIT`, and `//vars:CURRENT_TIME` each have different inputs selected at analysis time. Just because a file is an input to a rule doesn't mean it automatically gets used in actions at runtime. Bazel only works in the context of *inputs* and *outputs* of the action graph.

③ We mark the package as being publically visible since otherwise, we can't depend on its targets.

From this moment on, we can read individual variables. So let's change the implementation of our status rule to accommodate this. We need to change the of our rule from:

```
status = rule(
    implementation = _status,
)
```

to:

```python
status = rule(
  implementation = _status,
  attrs = {
    "_git_commit": attr.label(allow_single_file=True,
default="//vars:STABLE_GIT_COMMIT"),
    "_current_time": attr.label(allow_single_file=True,
default="//vars:CURRENT_TIME"),
  }
)
```

Of course, we update the implementation of the rule as well to reflect the changes:

```python
def _status(ctx):
  out = ctx.actions.declare_file(ctx.label.name)

  args = ctx.actions.args()
  args.add(ctx.file._git_commit)
  args.add(ctx.file._current_time)
  args.add(out)

  ctx.actions.run_shell(
    command="""
      echo "Project Status $(cat $1) built at $(cat $2)."
> $3
    """,
    arguments=[args],
    inputs=[ctx.file._git_commit,
ctx.file._current_time],
    outputs=[out])

  return [DefaultInfo(files=depset([out]))]
```

After we implemented this, you can change other stable variables, and you'll notice that the action doesn't change.

If you intend to have cross-platform builds, shell scripts will be problematic on windows. If that's the case, write your status script as a python script, and execute it with `--workspace_status_command="python bazel/status.py"`. Python is a required dependency of Bazel, and will be available on all platforms. Don't use shebangs (`#!/usr/bin/env python`), but use the `python` interpreter call, since Windows ignores shebangs when executing the file.

# 3.5. Assembling Builds Summary

In our quest for creating real builds, we looked first at macros, the simple functions that allow us to template and glue multiple rules together.

After that, we had a short look at the native rules bundled in Bazel: We started with `genrule` that simplifies the creation of targets that only depend on a script template. After, we mentioned the bundled native rules to process Java, C++, or Python code, and changed our compilation and linking to use the native `cc_binary` rule.

Then we looked at *packages and workspaces*, and how the `BUILD` and `WORKSPACE` files define them. We analyzed how *labels* can point to targets across different packages inside the same, or an external, workspace.

Next, to glue things together, we created a small project with a 7zip archival rule this time written in Java. The rule required external Maven dependencies. We did that to exercise external workspaces, and by extension, the external dependencies fetching from Bazel.

After, we wrote our own custom repository rule, that showed us how we could have external dependencies fetched on-demand, and how we can generate on the fly the folder structure and write our `BUILD` files for the external workspace.

Lastly, we went on how we can feed *external data* into our build, either via *environment variables* or via *a script executed by Bazel before our build*.

# Chapter 4. Appendix

# 4.1. Investigating Builds

As we can see, there can be quite some complexity in the Bazel builds. In investigating this, we'll look at how we can examine our builds overall, with the dependencies between the packages, and also how we can look inside a single package and trace what's happening there. Let's start with a single package.

## 4.1.1. Print

When writing the Skylark code, you might want to know what is the current state when doing the analysis part of the code. If that's the case, we can always go to the good old `print` statement.

```
print("compiling {} -> {}".format(f, out))
```

The messages you print here will appear in the Bazel log as DEBUG statements. In case there's a structure you don't know about, you can defer to the `dir` function that lists all the properties available on an object. For example, here's how we can list all the available properties on the action context:

```
def _print_context(ctx):
  print(dir(ctx))

  out = ctx.actions.declare_file("out")
  ctx.actions.write(output=out, content="")

  return [DefaultInfo(files=depset([out]))]

print_context = rule(
  implementation = _print_context,
)
```

This code would yield:

```
Loading:
Loading: 0 packages loaded
Analyzing: target //:print (0 packages loaded, 0 targets
configured)
DEBUG: /home/raptor/learn/projects/bazel-
book/code/rule_print_context/bazel/print_ctx.bzl:2:3:
["action", "actions", "aspect_ids", "attr", "bin_dir",
"build_file_path", "build_setting_value",
"check_placeholders", "configuration",
"coverage_instrumented", "created_actions",
"default_provider", "disabled_features", "empty_action",
"executable", "expand", "expand_location",
"expand_make_variables", "experimental_new_directory",
"features", "file", "file_action", "files", "fragments",
"genfiles_dir", "host_configuration", "host_fragments",
"info_file", "label", "new_file", "outputs",
"resolve_command", "resolve_tools", "rule", "runfiles",
"split_attr", "target_platform_has_constraint",
"template_action", "tokenize", "toolchains", "var",
"version_file", "workspace_name"]
INFO: Analyzed target //:print (0 packages loaded, 0
targets configured).
INFO: Found 1 target...
[0 / 1] [Prepa] BazelWorkspaceStatusAction stable-
status.txt
Target //:print up-to-date:
  bazel-bin/out
INFO: Elapsed time: 0.093s, Critical Path: 0.00s
INFO: 0 processes.
INFO: Build completed successfully, 1 total action
INFO: Build completed successfully, 1 total action
```

## 4.1.2. Query Packages

Now, it might be easy to commit a single package build into

memory, but what do we do with large projects? After all Bazel was designed for that, in having large projects in the first place, with a lot of dependencies. Of course, we understand now how its aggressive caching might help, but how can we use it? How can we look at the graph that's being built, and analyze what's going on?

Well, the good news is that Bazel offers us a command called `query` that, as its name states, allows us to query the graph of the dependencies between targets.

If we go to our archive example, we could investigate what do we need for us to get the `out.zip` file. Let's obtain the list of the dependent targets that we need, to get our output target:

```
//:out.zip
//:src/README.md
//:link
//:compile
//:src/print.h
//:src/print.c
//:src/main.c
```

This output looks pretty bland, but if we run it specifying the `--output` as `label_kind` we'll get more exciting results. Now it becomes also clearer where each target comes from:

```
$ bazel query "deps(out.zip)" --output label_kind
archive rule //:out.zip
source file //:src/README.md
link rule //:link
compile rule //:compile
source file //:src/print.h
source file //:src/print.c
source file //:src/main.c
```

Sometimes it's easier to look from afar at the package dependencies. We can use it at even a higher level, using the `package` output type, so we'd see only dependencies on other packages. Let's do that for our maven java project:

```
$ bazel query "deps(//project:data)" --output package
@bazel_tools//src/conditions
@bazel_tools//src/main/cpp/util
@bazel_tools//src/main/native/windows
@bazel_tools//src/tools/launcher
@bazel_tools//src/tools/launcher/util
@bazel_tools//third_party/def_parser
@bazel_tools//tools/build_defs/cc/whitelists/parse_header
s_and_layering_check
@bazel_tools//tools/cpp
@bazel_tools//tools/def_parser
@bazel_tools//tools/jdk
@bazel_tools//tools/launcher
@local_config_cc//
@local_jdk//
@maven//
@remote_java_tools_darwin//
@remote_java_tools_darwin//java_tools/zlib
@remote_java_tools_linux//
@remote_java_tools_linux//java_tools/zlib
@remote_java_tools_windows//
@remote_java_tools_windows//java_tools/zlib
@rules_jvm_external//private/templates
@rules_jvm_external//settings
bazel/archive
external
project
version
```

This is quite verbose. We can filter out external tooling using the `--notool_deps` flag. Everything that we use as a binary, including our java binary that we create for the 7zip archival gets pruned:

```
project
version
```

Now, in my opinion, one of the best output formats available is the `graph` output. This output is awesome because it shows us how the dependencies are, and we can easily the project structure and how the caching is working. Now, to be 100% honest, the `graph` output isn't outputting a graph image, but rather a graph definition that we can render using dot [https://graphviz.org/]. So let's do that:

```
bazel query "deps(//project:data)" --output graph
--notool_deps > graph.dot
```

The output of the `graph.dot` file is the dependency definition, from our project:

```
digraph mygraph {
  node [shape=box];
  "//project:data"
  "//project:data" ->
"//project:users.txt\n//project:groups.txt\n//version:dat
a.txt"

"//project:users.txt\n//project:groups.txt\n//version:dat
a.txt"
}
```

Using dot, we can render this graph:

```
dot -Tpng -Ograph.png graph.dot
```

If we open this image, this is what we'll see:

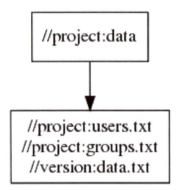

This image gives us a far more precise picture of what's going on. It might look bland here, but in non-trivial projects, where macros are stitching the rules together, this becomes an invaluable tool in untangling what's going on.

 Use the graph output to visualize dependencies between rules.

Now, as you probably have guessed from the `deps(out.zip)` this is a custom expression of some sort. The query accepts a Domain-Specific Language (DSL) where we spell out what we want to query. We can dump the full graph or analyze dependencies between targets.

We're not going to repeat the official documentation [https://docs.bazel.build/versions/master/query-how-to.html] here, instead, just be aware you can query questions such as "why does my dependency A depend on B," or "what's the path from target A to target B"?

# Chapter 5. Conclusion

*Thank you* for taking your time in reading Core Bazel. I mean it. It is an effort from your side that I am grateful for.

By now, you should understand how Bazel works, and we should have some answers for our initial quest: How does Bazel work internally? How do we create and extend Bazel builds?

We covered many things, but also I'm sure we missed quite a few in our effort to be concise and to the point.

Regardless, I think *something* is better than *nothing*, so instead of endlessly postponing this book, it's probably better to have it somewhat incomplete, and change it later, than never-ending it.

So if you feel there was something *core* that was missed, I apologize. It wasn't intentional. I just wanted to give you an introduction I wish I could have got when starting Bazel.

If you have any suggestions on doing this material better, please don't hesitate to contact me at bogdan.mustiata@gmail.com [mailto:bogdan.mustiata@gmail.com].

Enjoy your day, and build something amazing!

www.ingramcontent.com/pod-product-compliance
Lightning Source LLC
LaVergne TN
LVHW072049060326
832903LV00053B/304